AN EXERCISE IN NECROMANCY

Patrick Roche

BOWERY POETRY
an imprint of
the operating system
2017

BOWERY
ARTS +
SCIENCE

presents
the operating system print//document

AN EXERCISE IN NECROMANCY

ISBN 978-1-946031-14-3
Library of Congress Catalog Number 2017952077

copyright © 2017 by Patrick Roche
edited and designed by Lynne DeSilva-Johnson
cover art: Patte Loper, "Until I Hear You Sigh Here," 2009.

This book is released under a Creative Commons CC-BY-NC-ND
(Attribution, Non Commercial, No Derivatives) License:
its reproduction is encouraged for those who otherwise could not afford its
purchase in the case of academic, personal, and other creative usage from which
no profit will accrue.   Complete rules and restrictions are available at:

http://creativecommons.org/licenses/by-nc-nd/3.0/

For additional questions regarding reproduction, quotation, or to request a pdf
for review contact **operator@theoperatingsystem.org**

*This text was set in Avenir, Baskerville, Minion Pro, Phosphate and
OCR-A Standard, with distribution and POD via Ingram.*

BOWERY POETRY
is an imprint of
the operating system

http://theoperatingsystem.org | fb.com/thisistheoperatingsystem
http://bowerypoetry.com | fb.com/bowerypoetry | @bowerypoetry

AN EXERCISE IN NECROMANCY

TABLE OF CONTENTS

Annotated Guide to Raising the Dead - 7
Contrapuntal: Lazarus Taking My Antidepressants - 8
Icarus - 9
Suburbs in July - 11
Other Names I've Given to My Depression - 13
Hocus Pocus - 14

*In Which the Writer Meets His Father
for the First Time Since His Father's Death - 17*
Contrapuntal: Orpheus Is My Boyfriend - 20
Lafayette Street - 21
Neverland - 22
Contrapuntal: Narcissus Looking in My Mirror - 24
Ode to Streetlights - 25
Retcon - 27
Scheherazade - 29
Contrapuntal: Jesus Bring My Father - 31
Alchemy - 32
On Laying the Dead to Rest - 35
Ode to my Unread Messages - 37
Acknowledgements - 40
Poetics & Practice - 42

ANNOTATED GUIDE TO RAISING THE DEAD[1]

Identify the body[2] in question. The more recent the body, the better, but older ones will do just fine.[3] If possible, find one with an open mouth[4] and working tongue. Gather herbs and blood[5] to anoint the body. Wash the body in the blood[6] thoroughly.[7] Invoke appropriate deities[8] and demand that the body breathe again. As the body rises, ask the questions most pressing in your lungs. Brace for the answers, even the ones you'd rather leave buried.[9]

---

1 cf. Lucan, *Pharsalia*, Book VI; Apuleius, *The Golden Ass*, Book II; *Book of John* 11:1-44; *The Princess Bride*; et al.
2 Whether human, memory, song, voice, soul, unraveled quilt, elementary school time capsule, the author himself, or otherwise
3 Freshness of the dead can be determined by how easily the body recoils at the touch of the author or witch or past love, or by how comfortable the dirt has become, or by whether the body's mother can still be seen in its eyes
4 NB: you cannot open a mouth that is not there, or which you have already removed, unless you wish to slice a new mouth into the corpse altogether
5 Blood will always be more effective than the herbs. The author's blood will do, as it always has a way of spilling and staining a dead thing
6 Remind the body of how it once was alive and pulsing
7 If the blood is stubborn and will not come, dig deeper or look through old photographs or stand in the bathroom, naked
8 Whichever ones have not already forsaken you. Invent new ones if all other options have been exhausted
9 The dead will not lie. The dead are nothing if not a truth that will not blink.

LAZARUS

is a dead man
living or is
a rusted skeleton

crying to spite the inevitability
of earth

crying because
Messiah
this is what heaven looks like

four days later lying in the dark
how the body could be
wishing for life after tomb
rise and
breathe

TAKING MY ANTIDEPRESSANTS

laughing at the impossibility of
a deflated tire
aiming anywhere but a ditch,
anywhere but the cliff,

and
I'm still wishing to fly
they tell me these pills can help
me back from the brink if I just believe
in this littlest bottle of chemicals
I fail at reading
reflecting on such meager attempt at miracle
such small handful
wishing I could believe
for once

ICARUS
after Bastille

In the myth of Icarus and his father Daedalus,
Daedalus was a master craftsman
To save himself and Icarus from the Labyrinth on Crete
He built, by hand, wings out of wax and feathers
Mid-flight Icarus couldn't resist the warmth and the promise,
Flew too close to the sun, melted his wings, and fell to death in the sea

My father knew how to work with his hands
How to build
Said there was nothing that couldn't be fixed...with enough duct tape
Every Halloween we turned our front yard into a haunted house
Tombstones built out of wood and duct tape

My father loved haunting, loved horror and ghosts
He drank himself to death, drowned his liver, a ghastly flood

I was listed as his heir
I'm afraid my inheritance is one of waterlogged graves
My family knows how to build tombstones
How to fall to death in the sea

I'm 25, and I've never had a drink
Addiction and alcoholism, the rising tide in my veins
They are the duct tape wings my father built for me
I don't want to learn how to fly on them

I've never had alcohol, but I have tasted its warmth and promise
In the soaked air of parties
In the allure of a restaurant's wine list
On the tongues of my lovers
I kiss my boyfriend after he's had a glass of wine

And the sun erupts behind his teeth
A bartender spills a drink on me and
the ocean drags its salt across my skin
My friends offer me a beer in the heat of a college dorm room
And the wax, the duct tape, the feathers
start melting and peeling from my back

My alcoholic genetics are a thirsty beast clawing out of my mouth
For a glimpse of the sun
For a taste of the ocean breeze

Living as Icarus is exhausting, chasing my
Father's ghost through the clouds
Afraid of flying too high or too low, of falling to death in the sea
But I have my father's hazel eyes
My mother's brown couldn't quite keep out the sea-green glow
And now, every time I consider a glass of wine
They shine in the sunlight,
The wax melts,
The tide rolls in

SUBURBS IN JULY
after Rufus Wainwright's "Zebulon"

A Dunkin' Donuts is not the appropriate scene for an exhuming
Jonathan is back from Baltimore and I am back from the latest funeral or reminder of one, and I've ordered a hot chocolate in July because the last winter was as stubborn as I am and neither of us is willing to surrender my bones fully to the other
But Jonathan didn't come here to talk human anatomy or thermodynamics, just to catch up, even though I keep looking to his lips and remembering how he used to let me kiss him in high school when his \parents were out, even though he was my straight friend, and I don't think he felt anything then, at least nothing that would qualify as a poem in the right light, only pity for this boy in his arms who would wander to the dugouts down by the fields if it meant the dusty embrace of another boy (whose girlfriend didn't know any better, or did but didn't want to know)
And Jonathan was always the protective type so maybe he figured this was a noble sacrifice of skin to keep his friend from the kind of shadow and sandpaper love that conservative, working class suburbia offers queer kids
But Jonathan didn't come 200 miles to let me be a charity of sex this time. He just came to catch up and ask about Matt and Julia and my mother and my father and my grandparents and college and how my knees are doing since I busted them and can't run anymore.
And I sketch the outline of his jaw into my mind since I won't see him for a few more years after we leave and I say

They're all fine   or

they're the same, which is to say the opposite of the first statement,   or

half of them are dead and I've started to wonder how much money my family has donated to the tombstone maker's kids' college funds because maybe that's a consolation,   or *we try to put flowers and grave blankets out at Christmas and you'd think that would make the cemetery brighter but somehow it makes everything look worse,*   or

they said it snowed so much last winter it could cover fire hydrants,   or

I say nothing, because nobody in this Dunkin' Donuts asked to see a whole row of graves upturned all out in the open and loud like that, and Jonathan will be moving away and running half marathons in another city soon and I'll have a boyfriend and maybe nothing will stay dead in suburbia or maybe everything always will, and Jonathan says we should go get ice cream the next time he's in town
even though it will probably be winter.

OTHER NAMES I'VE GIVEN TO MY DEPRESSION

My mother's continued attendance at church

Chalk lining my throat

My therapist's source of income

I can't make it. I'm sorry to cancel again.

My own sluggish body, the rough draft of a suicide note

Rusty shovel, expectant grave

Lowered libido, delayed ejaculation

A face ghosting away from picture frames

I'm sorry.

Radio static

Just really busy.

The irrational fear of quicksand I gained from Saturday morning cartoons, a constant sinking, both slow and quick

A pistol

A rope

My father's hands

HOCUS POCUS

I love Hocus Pocus
Always have
The 90s Halloween movie—Bette Midler, Sarah Jessica Parker,
Kathy Najimy as Salem witches
As a child, watching the Sanderson sisters
consume the life force of their victims
Everyone would joke that
At least I'd never have to worry about that
The joke being that no one would want to eat me because I'm too thin

I ignored my urge to say
The witches weren't eating anyone, just sucking the energy out of children so they could maintain their youth, god were you paying attention at all
Instead, I laughed, proud that someone
Noticed how little space I could take up
I quickly learned that no one prods too much when you are all magic and party trick
Watch how much I can suck in my stomach! You can count every one of ribs and my vertebrae!
Bet you can fit your hand around my whole arm!

This body, the best show in town

It's so easy to tell someone you "forgot" to eat breakfast
If you word it the right way
I've learned every trick
How to hide the dark magic and only show the cape and confetti
Watch me regurgitate handkerchief after handkerchief
Watch me swallow fire and swords
And nothing else

I weighed myself every day
Conjured excuses for meals
Buried food in the garbage can
Down the drain

Into the napkin
The sleight of hand was the hardest part to master
I learned the telltale signs of disordered eating when I was a teenager
But as far as I could tell
Boys don't get that kind of sick
No one told me they could
We didn't have a name for that
But haven't we always been mystified by the nameless, the unknown
What we don't understand
Haven't we always called that magic?

What is more witchcraft than the way this body keeps moving forward
Even when I put nothing into it
Even when my hair falls out in the shower
Even when this body tells me every day it is dying or has died
But trudges still
What an abomination, what a mystery of nature
How should I name this? This dead thing I call a body
Or this body I called a dead thing
Buried day after day

If I start robbing my own grave
Begin a slow resurrection
Slice into the chicken breast instead of my silhouette
And swallow it all
Does that count? Have I started shoveling out the soil yet?
Have these lungs started to breathe in air
Or light
Or anything other than the dirt of their own grave?
Will it make any difference?
What do you call a body that can't hold anything, not even itself
But still tries to live?
Is this phoenix or undead, this body
An exercise in necromancy
Is it rebirth? Or is it just trying to make a zombie walk with the living?

I've tried eating regularly
I always give up after a few days
I assume this body is a lost cause
Too much torch and rot
Decaying taxidermy mounted on the wall
Rusted fossil
Ready for museum
Or morgue
Or freak show

Step right up
Keep your eyes peeled
You just might witness
The greatest disappearing act you've ever seen

Look!

It's happening right now

**IN WHICH THE WRITER MEETS HIS FATHER
FOR THE FIRST TIME SINCE HIS FATHER'S DEATH**

And he's just
Standing there
Like his feet have forgotten they aren't supposed to be stubborn anymore
And he can't hear my voice
Because my mouth is an ambulance siren
I wake up wailing in the dark
And I think it's my dad's name
And he's still standing there
In our old garage, the smell of rust and mold,
This ruined temple of things that should be dead but have
Resigned themselves to overgrowth
    Your car used to be right here
    Do you remember that car, dad?
    Do you remember this place, dad?
    When mom and I left, you told our neighbor to look for you here
    Said you were going to tie your belt to the rafters
    And finally give your stubborn feet a rest from the ground
    and all its unforgiving hard
    Dad, I know you were sick
    The neighbor called the sirens to come for you
    You said we did that to you
    Like you couldn't believe the betrayal
    Dad, did you forget I've always been a siren?
When he finally opens his mouth
Where his tongue should be
A pair of headlights careens forward
Every tooth a piece of gravel on the street where he was run over
After passing out in an alcoholic daze

He says my name but it's not my name
I don't understand his voice
When I say I don't understand his voice I mean
His voice is the sound of the car's brakes, I mean

His voice is the sound of ribs splintering and popping, I mean
His voice is the voice of the man driving the car
When I say his voice is the voice of the man driving the car, I mean
I don't know what my father's voice sounds like
When I say I don't know what my father's voice sounds like I mean
I don't know whether it still sounds like love or abuse or forgiveness or blame
Or a siren
I think it's the siren
I think he's speaking to me with my own voice. I mean
I don't understand my own voice

Dad, I'm sick, too
I told people to look for me in the rafters, too
I think they're coming for me, too, Dad
I hear the sirens when I dream
Or is that just you?
My therapist says I shouldn't turn you into a demon
You never believed in therapy
Dad, why are you still wearing that suit?
You couldn't even brush the dirt off after we buried you?
Why are we here?
Your cigarettes are still collecting in the corner by the rakes
Dad, that's probably dangerous. We keep cars in here
Dad, why are you so drawn to gasoline?
This place is still burning
We don't even call you dad anymore, just "him"
Just "remember the time he…" like you don't have a name
Or a body
You always liked ghost stories
Dad, we took down all the pictures of you
Dad, I hate this garage
Why are we here?
You couldn't stay sober long enough to teach me how to drive
Dad, I got into a car accident the other day

Dad, how do I stop blaming your grave for everything that goes up in

smoke?
How do I pull out of my garage and not see your hands on the steering wheel?
Dad, I never visited you in the hospital before you died
They said even while you were in a coma
Your body was going into withdrawal without the alcohol
Like it kept screaming in its sleep because it missed the thing that had broken it
Dad, I wake up to my own voice wailing sirens all the time
How long do withdrawal symptoms last?

ORPHEUS IS MY BOYFRIEND

a harp in his hands, lyrics
teaching the dead to sing
he is a gentle kind of summer
leading his love back from Hades
with
trust in his wake
he tries against logic
or at least hopes
not
to look back at the ghost

happy, a trumpet of smile
in spite of all my empty and sick
or is he

uncertain steps but only
not leaving
because he knows
I will
be afraid
of my past and of the lonely hauntings
to come

LAFAYETTE STREET

On my way from the Nuyorican Poets Café to my boyfriend's apartment
I'm walking on Lafayette Street
When a man confronts me, *"Where you going, princess?"*
When I don't acknowledge him at all, he shouts,
"Faggot pussy bitch"
And I should have been angry
But internalized homophobia is quite the saboteur
So I spent the next three days
Wondering where I slipped up
Too often, young queer people have to learn to hide their own names,
Remove the switch in their step,
Blend into the wallpaper
So where had I failed in this chameleon training? How could he tell?
Maybe he looked into my mouth, saw the quivering tongue,
afraid of betraying
Years of speech therapy to straighten my lisp
Maybe he saw the anchors I fix to my wrists to make them anything
but limp
Maybe he saw through the masks I've built ever since I realized
Sometimes it's safer in costume
Maybe he just thought that was the worst thing he could call me
Like he had chewed up my name and
Spat out new ones for me—*faggot, pussy, bitch*
Or maybe, maybe he could smell the child fermenting in my own shame
That child who didn't know the meaning of shame
That child who only answered to his own name
That child, even now, rotting away somewhere inside me

NEVERLAND

"I am jealous of everything whose beauty does not die" - Oscar Wilde

When my boyfriend shaves my ass, just after he's finished
Sculpting my pubic hair into whatever
Tame he finds satisfactory
In the same breath, he tells me I look so hot like this
And assures me it's not because I look like a child or prepubescent
or slick linoleum

The tissues in his trash can
Are stiffening
With bits of us we emptied last night
Watching two twinks on his laptop
Undo each other's belts
Pants
Tongues
Eyes
I think they were supposed to be summer camp friends
Or step-brothers
Or a Justin Bieber lookalike and a fan's dripping teeth
I guess in the end it doesn't matter
The point is, none of them had body hair

How long did Peter Pan wait before he kicked out his boys?
Was it the first weed cracking through
The stubborn cement under their tunic?
Was it the day one forgot to shave
His upper lip?

My boyfriend tells me it looks better—not better, but
Really nice—this way
And I want to ask him if he only dated me because he thought
I looked younger on my profile
But I let him compliment this smooth, this

Ritual grooming, this calmed
Riot of hair
Because I agree: it looks better this way
And this was my idea in the first place
So I should be okay with all of this, this refusal of age, this body
        sculpted jailbait
After all, twink is the first word in all of my porn searches
And now there are no rude tangles interfering with
His tongue later that night
So what does it matter if I bury myself in this body
What does it matter if my skin clings to
Its childhood and tries to fly
What does it matter if I drown in whatever youth
Is desirable to other men
As long as I never age, never be anything but beautiful and smooth
        and statue
What does it matter if I become a lost boy
As long as no one finds me as a man
Right?

NARCISSUS

shuts out the world
thinks to himself
so pretty or
a lifelong love
wasting away into
nothing
trying to grab hold of
body
now
becoming a soft flower
in the mud

LOOKING IN MY MIRROR

seeing the boy's pallor
no one would say this is
worth
all that time and
dark
I'm often, perhaps, too vocal about
my depression and all this sad
but
sometimes I wonder if it might be better
becoming a more palatable kind of fragile

> *Cause you make me feel like*
> *I could be drivin' you all night*
> *And I'll find your lips in the streetlights*
> *I wanna be there with you*
> —Carly Rae Jepsen,
> "Run Away With Me"

ODE TO STREETLIGHTS
after Carly Rae Jepsen

Because who among us hasn't found a lover's lips to be a gentle glow
parting all shadow
in the kiss of the December city, respite from cement and iron and night
or in the soft rebellion of sex in a train station parking lot,
awkward fumbling over seat belts and suburban sweat
You, constant heat of defiance. You, shower of spotlights. You,
slow dance silhouette. You, showcase spectacle of my boyfriend
and me making a firework dance in our mouths on the street corner
You, reason for my fears when a man sees us. But
You maybe, also, reason for our safety. Hopefully
You, beacon of home and harbor

Come, see how this dusty flickering lamp has room for us
Holds us close. Will not succumb to the blanket of darkness
Will not sleep. Will not be anything but loud and here

I am afraid.
My boyfriend and I walk back from dinner and stay on the well-lit
path, but I worry that won't be enough. Still, I will not make this the sad
poem where I fade into the alleys or where
my shadow becomes a more central character than me
This is a celebration
Of a mother's wisdom in a curfew of lamplight
Of finding that comfort and safety in a lover's arms
Of how he mirrors the wash of dim yellow soaking
through the bedroom window

Hallelujah to a sweet escape from the fear of a stranger's rage or from the midnight fog
of my own sick mind
Hallelujah to finding that escape wherever it may lie--in the warm breath of fluorescence
or in the warm breath of a boy's palms. Either way, Hallelujah to these little mimics of sun
Small orbits of comfort
Hallelujah to the lighthouses on every corner and the light of a boy's eyes
Hallelujah to the streetlights painting the entire city into a map of my lover's face
Hallelujah to warm blood and the joy of a queer love, or at least a small hope of safety for it,
however meager
Hallelujah to running away into that safety with a smile and feeling home, if only briefly
Fighting back the dark and the sad and the fear and the depression and the cruel, if only briefly
Watch how this city cradles and kisses us in the light
And watch me fight for that, fight for finding joy in whatever brightness may fall on us
Watch me fight and watch me fight and watch me fight and watch me fight
And watch me kiss this city back so hard it never stops shining

RETCON

Retcon, as in
Retroactive continuity, is
A phenomenon common in comic books and television
In which writers alter previously canon storylines to fill plot holes
Or resurrect characters who were killed off
By retroactively adding to, completely erasing, or ignoring plot points that had, until this point,
Been set in stone

For example
In this issue, we learn that Jean Grey did not die as The Phoenix but was replicated and kept alive
Or in this issue, The Winter Soldier is revealed to be Bucky Barnes, returned to readers 50 years after his death
Or in this issue, we find that my father was replaced 10 years ago by Mystique, and he returns to us now without a glaze on his eyes
Or in this issue, my grandparents' cancer was just a parasite, now removed and jettisoned into space
Or my grandfather did not die on the same day as Whitney Houston
Or my mother no longer changes the station every time one of her songs comes on
Or my grandmother reveals her death as an elaborate ruse
Or in this issue, my other grandmother's dementia hasn't been retconning her life for the past 3 years, rewriting her husband as still alive or her children as someone else's blood or herself as anything but the good face in the mirror
Or in this issue, no one buried their child, or no one put down the dog, or no one colored their skin with a knife, or no one dreamt of a world washed clean of their stain

Or in this issue, I am not no one.
My mother is not no one
Or no one is no one
Or in this issue, the white walls and the hospital bed were just a dream, or illusion, or hypnotism
Or in this issue, without explanation, I no longer need the medicine
Or in this issue, I am The Phoenix
Or I relearn the language of a smile
Or I think of what a luxury it would be to erase, or revive, or reset, at the stroke of a pen
Or in this issue, I wonder how many deaths a story needs before it can be retconned
Or in this issue, I do not fear a death that I can return from
Or in this issue, I do not mourn anyone who never seems to stay dead
Or in this issue
Or in this issue
Or in this issue, I wait
And wait
For someone to rewrite me into a story with fewer holes

SCHEHERAZADE
after Richard Siken

And in this dream I have no tongue but he asks me to tell him the story
The one where I pull my body from the whirlpool and bring it back
from the dead
Or the one where I was drowning until I wasn't. Until my legs went
quiet and
My mind stopped flailing
Or the one where I let the boy slip his fingers into my waistband even
though I
Spent the day folded into the dark and would not eat
Except that is this story, happening now
And he then slips his tongue into my mouth
But remember
I didn't have a tongue, so what was I to do?
Isn't this how I pull my body back? Stop sinking
Into the night? Isn't that the way
You prove you're alive? By becoming a lagoon
A boy dives into instead of being
The same dead thing you've been
For the past five days? Isn't that life?
Being of use to another boy?

I do not tell the boy this. I do not tell him he has a corpse in his bed or that
He kissed bloodless lips. I do not tell him I've been
Depressed this week and haven't eaten
But for some reason still have enough
Of a sex drive to run a hand along his chest
I do not tell him this

I tell him the stories
A thousand of them
About how I breathed once
And rode a roller coaster once
And held a koala once

I tell him the stories about how I was alive
As if to remind myself I can be
But is he even listening?
I don't have a tongue, lest we forget. I dropped it
In the gutter or forgot it
In the drawer or swallowed it with the pills
But I have to tell him these stories
Every night
For 1000 nights, or 1001 if that's what it takes
For me to stop being dead
For me to begin to feel again
Something, anything, even if that is only his hands
And the small solace of sex
The only thing that reminds me some days
I still have a nervous system and
A heartbeat, when it races
Is that so shameful? Is that such a
Wrong comfort? Something that I should regret? That
He slips his tongue into my mouth again
And for a moment
I breathe

JESUS	**BRING MY FATHER**
returned from the grave	put the casket out
to dry	let his children
the world	and his family see how a body echoes
of its	life until funeral
tears	raise the prayer
or at least	his name
to say	look how
I will not leave you again	this family mourns too much

ALCHEMY

Last night I sat cross-legged on the bathroom tile
Turning the knife over in my hands, debating
The physics of its serrated edge
Watching the silver turn gold in the fluorescent light
This is not the poem where I used it to trace the lineage
Of my arteries until my father's face spilled from my wrist
Or where I practiced bladepoint calligraphy

This is the poem about how I wanted to kill myself
This is the poem about how I still want to kill myself
And I'm tired of turning that into something pretty
There is nothing pretty here
There is only the vomit this morning when I tried
To write this poem and instead found nausea
How I watched the ugliest parts of me work their way out
How I tried reflecting on the desire to pull out my blood, invert life
So my stomach followed suit, reversed itself, decided
If I couldn't commit to the blood
Acid would do

This is not the poem where I am the alchemist
Where I mix the dull into magic and miracle
Where I spin my blood into gold
A more worthwhile tragedy
For myself
For you

So we can hang it on the wall and discuss how beautifully it catches the light
Or makes all the lights disappear
So I don't have to confront the reality
I've written those poems
With the gold and the mirrors
But still couldn't transfigure the trauma
I can make it sing
But the trauma is still there after

So I won't hide this under magic anymore
This is no blood sacrifice for rebirth
This is just blood
This is just a lot of blood
Railing against itself
This is the stubborn surface
Tension of my skin. This is I
Forgot to take the medicine. This is I didn't
Forget to take the medicine. I just didn't take it.
This is I took the medicine. This is the medicine
Might not be working anymore. This is

I only stopped myself because I was scared
Or because I was ashamed
Or because my mother came home early
I heard the front door bolt click open
So I snuck out of the bathroom, returned the knife
To the kitchen drawer
My mother doesn't know about this
This is not the poem about hugs and a tearful resolution
This is the poem about how I tucked away the knife with
All of the dark and hoped it would stay hidden from everyone
This is the poem about shame
About sitting in a bathroom, wondering who
Will clean the red stains out of the grout

And I know
I said I wouldn't turn this into something pretty
I said there would be no alchemy
But no matter how much I say that,
Here I am, with a mouth full of gold,
Still wanting to kill myself, but not
Wanting to kill myself
And I don't know if there's a term or a poem for all that
So I'll settle for this, and hope it helps me peel away the shame or take a step forward
I'll settle for this
This poem, this small hope of words
This hope
      This body

This step

           This small

      This

ON LAYING THE DEAD TO REST

***

Fuck if I know how

***

Fido's ashes still sit in the carved wooden box
A picture of him perched on top of it
Displayed on the trunk just as you enter our apartment
He's lying on his bed, rawhide at his feet,
Looking at the camera, or, more accurately,
At me as I took the picture
My mother frequently reminds my brother and me
That we have to bury the box of ashes and the picture with her
When she dies

***

I don't remember what I put in the time capsule
We buried in 2nd grade
Maybe a Pokemon card?
I do remember watching the dirt fall and pile
I don't think anyone is going to dig it up

***

My boyfriend opens his laptop
Plays the latest episode
Of another zombie-pandemic-virus-apocalypse show
Splashing the screen with blood and the undead

He asks if I want to watch
I opt for petting his dog
***

My mother assumes she will be buried before me
***

I didn't attend my first wake until well into my teenage years
My first funeral even later than that
Even when it was within my own family,
I was conveniently busy with nothing in particular
I only knew people dying in theory
***

I criticize my mother for never throwing anything away
There is a box of Little League participation trophies in our garage
Next to the box of my old stuffed animals and baby blanket
I can't part with
Genetics breed a funny hypocrisy
***

I didn't cry over Mufasa
I didn't cry at any funerals I've attended
I don't know how to soften a grave
***

I take my sleeping pills and wait
For the minutes to pass so that they can take effect
I wouldn't care if they were just placebo
As long as I can sleep
I lay my head down
Lay myself to rest, or hope to
My nightly ritual in futility
Ritual in burial
***

Fuck if I know how

ODE TO MY UNREAD MESSAGES

Chorus of ghostly voices tucked into my pocket
Preservation behind thin pane of glass
Butterfly wings still fluttering with a whisper of breath
Of life, of friend, of family,
Of "haven't heard from you in a while"
Of "omg please watch this. Tell me this video isn't literally me"
Of "are you around this weekend? I'll be in town"

I am well practiced in the magic of levitation—how to leave a word floating
Untouched in the air, the weight of expectation boring a hole in my pant leg
With each vibration, tense reminder of existence without acknowledgment
It is not a skill I am proud of—of becoming a wishing well my friends toss
Coins into, wondering how long until they'll hear the metal hit water or
      rock or anything
Resembling echo, at least, if not response

My brain is a silly thing, hypocritical clown
It craves reassurance, validation, reminders of a voice that does not exist
      within its own walls
But also bathes itself in fear daily
In plain terms, my anxiety often destroys my simple capacity for interaction
Even for communication I myself initiate, it will not give me the strength
      to open a message
Which could say "hi" or "cool sounds good"
But could just as easily be a declaration of hatred or annoyance or word
that someone has died or that I am not welcome in the most basic areas of
      a person's heart

But those thoughts don't usually happen so distinctly. Often it is
Nothing more than an incessant screech of no. Of indefinable, wordless terror.

So I sit here with dozens, hundreds, thousands if you count spam—
    a small nation of
Screams in my inbox that I wish I had the strength to answer. And I know
    how stupid
That sounds, how easy it should be to press a button or even just
Delete. But somehow the knowledge of the simplicity only makes this harder

So my phone grows heavier and heavier, heavy with
An albatross of words, heavy with apologies I should be offering, heavy
With the faces of everyone I love and their voices that I may forget if I
    don't start
Listening, but heavy too with
Hope

With each message, each notification, a steady river of humanity. Hope
And wonder
At how I am offered life
and hands
and the smallest but sturdiest thread to grasp
And pull upward back into the light
How love lives here for me even in my absence, how people say
"We are here, and we know you are here
And we refuse to let anyone forget that, including you
So we will keep throwing you life vests until you come crawling into this
world again
Or anew
As if born free and clean"

And upon my second birth, we will tell everyone how I was caught and cradled in
So many arms and so many words and so many voices
We will tell them I am loved
Tell them I have an entire language-worth of praise and family
And we will keep telling them until it is the only fact I know of joy
And I will keep telling myself until it is the only fact I know
Of new life

ACKNOWLEDGMENTS

Thanks to anyone and everyone
who helped make this chapbook possible, including:

Bowery Poetry, Bowery Arts & Sciences, Nikhil Melnechuk, Bob Holman, Mason Granger and all the staff at Bowery for providing a space and community for poetry and emotion, and for believing in my work enough to let me contribute to their wonderful history

The Operating System and especially Lynne DeSilva-Johnson for their tireless work, help, and guidance in creating a product that brings my poems to a new height I could not have imagined

Ashley August for helming Bowery Slam in a way that fosters art and friendship, and for being the best future R&B music video star

The rest of the 2017 Bowery Slam Team (Timothy DuWhite, Joel Francois, Golden) for pushing me to be a better person and writer, for being willing to share space onstage, offstage, and in poems, and for being a kickass bowling team

The 2016 Union Square Slam Team (Kearah Armonie, Nkosi Nkululeko, Taylor Steele, our coach Cecily Schuler) and everyone else at Union Square Slam (Thomas Fucaloro, I.S. Jones, Rachel Simons, Sara Emily Kuntz, and others I'm sure I'm forgetting) for letting me cry and grow and share my stories alongside them, for road trips and Rent music, and for matching outfits

The Loser Slam and Jersey City Slam communities for giving me space in my own home state to feel welcome and heard

Friends who have looked over these poems and reassured me they weren't garbage (or told me when they were, because sometimes tough love is necessary), including Namkyu Oh, Aron Wander, Julian Randall, Jess Myers, all my teammates and colleagues mentioned above, and more

The staff at Vivi Bubble Tea who have memorized my order after spending countless hours writing and having emotional breakthroughs in their cafe

Peter, for believing in me and throwing himself into a strange world of poetry and scores and tears and love, and to the Liebenson/Selden family and Roscoe for being a warm and welcoming space in this city when I've needed a sense of calm and joy, and for helping me be a smart businessman

My mother, my brother, my sister-in-law, and all my family and friends for believing that I could succeed and that I have stories worth telling, for helping me become a better version of myself every day, and for always loving me more than I thought possible

PATRICK ROCHE is a poet, mental health advocate, and Carly Rae Jepsen enthusiast from New Jersey. Patrick has competed and featured at multiple national and international slam competitions, recently placing 3rd overall at the 2016 Individual World Poetry Slam. He serves as an ambassador for the JED Foundation, promoting mental and emotional wellness, suicide prevention, and substance abuse awareness among colleges and high schools. Patrick has performed alongside or shared stages with Darryl "DMC" McDaniels, Brittany Snow, Tyler James Williams, Chamique Holdsclaw, and many others. Patrick graduated in 2014 from Princeton University, where he began performing as part of Princeton's first spoken word poetry group, Ellipses. Videos of his work have amassed over 6 million views, and his work has been published or featured in *Beech Street Review, Voicemail Poems, Freezeray Press, Button Poetry, SlamFind, UpWorthy, Buzzfeed*, and his mom's fridge.

ABOUT THE ARTIST: PATTE LOPER

Patte Loper is a painter who experiments with sculpture and video. She was born in Colorado and grew up in Tallahassee, Florida, a subtropical college town where she first developed an appreciation for the ways nature and culture can overlap. She currently lives and works in Brooklyn, NY and Boston, MA where she is on the faculty of the School of the Museum of fine Arts at Tufts University.

She has shown her work in numerous solo and group exhibitions internationally, including the Drawing Center in New York, The Bronx Museum, The Licini Museum in Ascoli Piceno, Italy, LMCC's Art Center on Governor's Island New York, the Juliette Art Museum at the Clay Center for the Arts and Sciences, the PalaentologicalMuseum in Cortina, Italy, the Tacoma Art Museum, Suyama Space in Seattle, WA, and the Zuckerman Museum in Atlanta, GA. Her work has been reviewed in the Italian edition of Flash Art, Artnet, Time Out, Chicago, and the Boston Globe, and is in the collections of the Rene di Rosa Foundation, the Microsoft Corporation, and the Hirshhorn Museum.

The painting that graces the cover, "Until I Hear You Sigh Here," (2009), is Acrylic and Oil on Paper, 20" x 25," and is used with permission.

Find more of Patte and her work at: http://patteloper.com

POETICS and PROCESS

Patrick Roche in conversation with Lynne DeSilva-Johnson

Hey Patrick! Will you introduce yourself to our readers?

I'm Patrick Roche, a poet and mental health advocate who has spent my entire life in New Jersey, though I've become more attached to New York City in recent years. I'm also a huge fan of chocolate, pop music, video games, or any combination of those.

Why are you a poet / when did you decide you were a poet (and/or: do you feel comfortable calling yourself a poet, what other titles or affiliations do you prefer/feel are more accurate)? And, what's a "poet", anyway?

I am a poet out of luck and circumstance as much as I am one out of necessity. I wrote poetry occasionally throughout high school, but it became my primary means of escape and relief in college. I had injured my knees, so I no longer had the ability to go on runs, which had always helped clear my head. Just as I was turning to poetry more, a spoken word student group had started on campus, and through a series of open mic readings (at the strong urging of some friends), I crossed paths with that group. Once I became part of a community of writers, I fell in love with poetry even more and became fascinated with the impact that it can have on others. I needed a way to make sense of my experiences and the world around me, which I think is the closest to a working definition of a "poet" that I use for my own purposes. I've always felt a desire for clarity in my experiences, and I used to find that through running and allowing my thoughts to quiet. When I no longer had that, I decided to explore my experiences more directly, making sense of them and articulating their complexities with words. I continue to do this as much for my own selfish use (to cope with or process life) as I do to create dialogue and engage with an audience.

What is the role of the poet today? What do you see as your cultural and social role (in the poetry community and beyond)?

I think a very basic role of the poet has remained somewhat similar over the years—articulating those things which are difficult to pinpoint or exploring the human experience in a way that makes sense of the world. Today, we live in a remarkable age of having limitless information available to us and of seeing constant innovation and change (technological, political, social, medical, scientific). Finding the words to articulate how all of these experiences affect our lives, our emotions, our dreams, and our place in the world—that seems to be something that people need from writers and poets. The poet today has the ability to connect with people on a very visceral level, creating emotional bonds and sparking dialogue and thought, all in a time when those kinds of connections are increasingly difficult to forge.

Today, any artistic creation seems to be a political act given the pressures against art and artists. The poet today has been thrust into a political position by virtue of creating art at all. I hope to push myself further in that role by engaging with audiences in as genuine and authentic a way as possible. I have found that I am most effective and powerful when I speak from personal narrative, and I try to use those strengths to call attention to the importance of each individual person's stories and narratives—reclaiming our stories, realizing the strength of our experience. I also hope to serve as a voice to combat the stigma facing people with mental illness. I have found that articulating personal experiences with mental illness can be the most effective way of helping audiences understand those struggles.

Talk about the process or instinct to move these poems (or your work in general) as independent entities into a body of work. How and why did this happen? Have you had this intention for a while? What encouraged and/or confounded this (or a book, in general) coming together? Was it a struggle? Did you envision this collection as a collection or understand your process as writing specifically around a theme while the poems themselves were being written? How or how not?

I had written a few of the poems in this book over a short period of time about a year ago, but I did not consciously think about creating a cohesive collection or body of work. After I finished writing a few of them and started editing them or memorizing them for performance, I realized that there were common threads that ran through them—themes of rebirth, magic, life, memory, grief, acceptance.

I decided that I would try an exercise of writing more poems involving these themes, applying them to different experiences and topics or exploring different forms and styles. I had hoped I would end up with enough poems for a chapbook or some sort of collection, and I gradually reached a point of being satisfied with the poems as a body of work. I found the idea of rebirth to be very appealing, and as I wrote more, it felt cathartic and healing. Those feelings encouraged me to pursue these themes even more until I felt satisfied with the collection.

What formal structures or other constrictive practices (if any) do you use in the creation of your work? Have certain teachers or instructive environments, or readings/writings of other creative people (poets or others) informed the way you work/write?

Sometimes I am struck by a specific idea or subject and begin to write a poem from that point. Other times, I decide that I want to write in a specific form (as with the contrapuntals in this chapbook). I do not have a consistent pattern by any means. Recently, I've been most productive when I have tried an exercise of writing odes.

If I feel like I am in a creative slump, operating within a specific structure or form is helpful to me. I also look to the writing of as many different writers as I can, but I most often come back to people in my own communities. I have found so much inspiration from just sitting in the audience at an open mic or a slam in the area and being moved by people sharing their work with one another. Also, for some reason that I still can't figure out, the one physical environment that works best for me is a specific bubble tea shop? I don't know why I'm so productive there, but I'm not going to question it.

Speaking of monikers, what does your title represent? How was it generated? Talk about the way you titled the book, and how your process of naming (poems, sections, etc) influences you and/or colors your work specifically.

The title of this chapbook comes from a line in one of my poems, "Hocus Pocus." That poem (and a couple others that I wrote around the same time) made me realize how much I was writing about rebirth and magic. That specific line, "This body, an exercise in necromancy," sparked quite a few other poems and was in many ways the inspiration for crafting a collection around that idea.

What does this particular collection of poems represent to you
…as indicative of your method/creative practice?
…as indicative of your history?
…as indicative of your mission/intentions/hopes/plans?

This collection represents a shift in my writing toward a more cohesive, complex, and deliberate approach. But most importantly to me, it represents a slow shift toward healing and optimism. While many poems delve into some dark places (which I think are super necessary, and I am proud that I have found a way to articulate really difficult and painful experiences and thoughts), as the collection proceeds toward a point of acceptance (largely aided by writing odes), I think the collection marks a shift in my writing as a whole.

The collection also serves as a means for me to show the intersections of all of my experiences with family, mental health, love, and self-image. I hope that these poems will help me push myself even further in my role as someone who can engage with others on a personal level while speaking unashamedly about mental illness.

What does this book DO (as much as what it says or contains)?

This book speaks about everything I have felt ashamed of for very long. This book helps heal that shame, and hopefully it shows that personal narrative is one of the most meaningful and effective ways to connect with others.

What would be the best possible outcome for this book? What might it do in the world, and how will its presence as an object facilitate your creative role in your community and beyond? What are your hopes for this book, and for your practice?

I hope that people respond well to this book on an emotional level. I hope that it builds bridges and impacts those that read it, and I hope that it provides me with a platform for speaking with audiences and engaging in the kinds of dialogue that the book hopefully sparks— about hope, joy, mental illness, fear, sadness. I want to be a poet who can engage in conversations that explore how we can deconstruct stigma and shame. I hope this book helps me do that.

Let's talk a little bit about the role of poetics and creative community in social activism, in particular in what I call "Civil Rights 2.0," which has remained immediately present all around us in the time leading up to this series' publication. I'd be curious to hear some thoughts on the challenges we face in speaking and publishing across lines of race, age, privilege, social/cultural background, and sexuality within the community, vs. the dangers of remaining and producing in isolated "silos.

I fell in love with poetry because of its ability to connect and create conversations, especially those that involve examinations of social issues, race, gender, age, privilege, etc…and as I alluded to above, speaking openly and creating art have become political acts in and of themselves. Therefore, I feel a need to place poetics (especially the poetry I share, which so often involves speaking to audiences and engaging with a community) within the context of our current political climate, creating space for progress and social change that shows, listens to, celebrates, amplifies, and engages with marginalized voices.

 **& the operating system**

IN COLLABORATION

The Operating System is pleased to announce the new Bowery Poetry imprint, in collaboration with Bowery Arts + Science, a series beginning with the book you hold in your hands, *An Exercise in Necromancy,* by Patrick Roche.

Bowery Poetry is a project of Bowery Arts+Science, a 501(c)3 non-profit in New York City, USA. Our mission is to encourage cooperation among and advancement of artists and cultural workers; to develop and produce works by emerging poets and performers; and to promote the exploration, improvement, and advancement of the arts as a changemaking force in society.

Bowery Poetry's Chapbook Slam is an annual competition where poets face off at Bowery Slam for a chance to have their work published. Patrick Roche is the Chapbook Slam's first winner.

Congratulations Patrick!

WHY PRINT / DOCUMENT?

The Operating System uses the language "print document" to differentiate from the book-object as part of our mission to distinguish the act of documentation-in-book-FORM from the act of publishing as a backwards facing replication of the book's agentive *role* as it may have appeared the last several centuries of its history. Ultimately, I approach the book as TECHNOLOGY: one of a variety of printed documents (in this case bound) that humans have invented and in turn used to archive and disseminate ideas, beliefs, stories, and other evidence of production.

Ownership and use of printing presses and access to (or restriction of printed materials) has long been a site of struggle, related in many ways to revolutionary activity and the fight for civil rights and free speech all over the world. While (in many countries) the contemporary quotidian landscape has indeed drastically shifted in its access to platforms for sharing information and in the widespread ability to "publish" digitally, even with extremely limited resources, the importance of publication on physical media has not diminished. In fact, this may be the most critical time in recent history for activist groups, artists, and others to insist upon learning, establishing, and encouraging personal and community documentation practices.

With The OS's print endeavors I wanted to open up a conversation about this: the ultimately radical, transgressive act of creating PRINT /DOCUMENTATION in the digital age. It's a question of the archive, and of history: who gets to tell the story, and what evidence of our life, our behaviors, our experiences are we leaving behind? We can know little to nothing about the future into which we're leaving an unprecedentedly digital document trail — but we can be assured that publications, government agencies, museums, schools, and other institutional powers that be will continue to leave BOTH a digital and print version of their production for the official record. Will we?

As a (rogue) anthropologist and long time academic, I can easily pull up many accounts about how lives, behaviors, experiences — how THE STORY of a time or place — was pieced together using the deep study of correspondence, notebooks, and other physical documents which are no longer the norm in many lives and practices. As we move our creative behaviors towards digital note taking, and even audio and video, what can we predict about future technology that is in any way assuring that our stories will be accurately told – or told at all? How will we leave these things for the record?

In these documents we say:
WE WERE HERE, WE EXISTED, WE HAVE A DIFFERENT STORY

- Lynne DeSilva-Johnson, Founder/Managing Editor,
THE OPERATING SYSTEM, Brooklyn NY 2016

TITLES IN THE PRINT: DOCUMENT COLLECTION

An Absence So Great and Spontaneous It Is Evidence of Light - Anne Gorrick [2018]
Chlorosis - Michael Flatt and Derrick Mund [2018]
Sussuros a Mi Padre - Erick Sáenz [2018]
Sharing Plastic - Blake Nemec [2018]
The Book of Sounds - Mehdi Navid (trans. Tina Rahimi) [2018]
Abandoners - Lesley Ann Wheeler [2018]
Jazzercise is a Language - Gabriel Ojeda-Sague [2018]
Death is a Festival - Anis Shivani [2018]
Return Trip / Viaje Al Regreso; Dual Language Edition -
Israel Dominguez,(trans. Margaret Randall) [2018]
Born Again - Ivy Johnson [2018]
Singing for Nothing - Wally Swist [2018]
One More Revolution - Andrea Mazzariello [2017]
Fugue State Beach - Filip Marinovich [2017]
Lost City Hydrothermal Field - Peter Milne Greiner [2017]
The Book of Everyday Instruction - Chloe Bass [2017]
In Corpore Sano : Creative Practice and the Challenged Body
[Anthology, 2017] Lynne DeSilva-Johnson and Jay Besemer, co-editors
Love, Robot - Margaret Rhee[2017]
La Comandante Maya - Rita Valdivia (tr. Margaret Randall) [2017]
The Furies - William Considine [2017]
Nothing Is Wasted - Shabnam Piryaei [2017]
Mary of the Seas - Joanna C. Valente [2017]
Secret-Telling Bones - Jessica Tyner Mehta [2017]
CHAPBOOK SERIES 2017 : INCANTATIONS
featuring original cover art by Barbara Byers
sp. - Susan Charkes; Radio Poems - Jeffrey Cyphers Wright; Fixing a Witch/
Hexing the Stitch - Jacklyn Janeksela; cosmos a personal voyage by carl sagan ann
druyan steven sotor and me - Connie Mae Oliver
Flower World Variations, Expanded Edition/Reissue - Jerome
Rothenberg and Harold Cohen [2017]
Island - Tom Haviv [2017]
What the Werewolf Told Them / Lo Que Les Dijo El Licantropo -
Chely Lima (trans. Margaret Randall) [2017]
The Color She Gave Gravity - Stephanie Heit [2017]
The Science of Things Familiar - Johnny Damm [Graphic Hybrid, 2017]

agon - Judith Goldman [2017]
To Have Been There Then / Estar Alli Entonces - Gregory Randall
(trans. Margaret Randall) [2017]
Instructions Within - Ashraf Fayadh [2016]
Arabic-English dual language edition; Mona Kareem, translator
Let it Die Hungry - Caits Meissner [2016]
A GUN SHOW - Adam Sliwinski and Lynne DeSilva-Johnson;
So Percussion in Performance with Ain Gordon and Emily Johnson [2016]
Everybody's Automat [2016] - Mark Gurarie
How to Survive the Coming Collapse of Civilization [2016] - Sparrow
CHAPBOOK SERIES 2016: OF SOUND MIND
*featuring the quilt drawings of Daphne Taylor
Improper Maps - Alex Crowley; While Listening - Alaina Ferris;
Chords - Peter Longofono; Any Seam or Needlework - Stanford Cheung
TEN FOUR - Poems, Translations, Variations [2015] - Jerome Rothenberg,
Ariel Resnikoff, Mikhl Likht (w/ Stephen Ross)
MARILYN [2015] - Amanda Ngoho Reavey

CHAPBOOK SERIES 2015: OF SYSTEMS OF
*featuring original cover art by Emma Steinkraus
Cyclorama - Davy Knittle; The Sensitive Boy Slumber Party Manifesto
- Joseph Cuillier; Neptune Court - Anton Yakovlev; Schema - Anurak Saelow
SAY/MIRROR [2015; 2nd edition 2016] - JP HOWARD
Moons Of Jupiter/Tales From The Schminke Tub [plays, 2014] - Steve Danziger

CHAPBOOK SERIES 2014: BY HAND
Pull, A Ballad - Maryam Parhizkar; Can You See that Sound - Jeff Musillo
Executive Producer Chris Carter - Peter Milne Grenier;
Spooky Action at a Distance - Gregory Crosby;

CHAPBOOK SERIES 2013: WOODBLOCK
*featuring original prints from Kevin William Reed
Strange Coherence - Bill Considine; The Sword of Things - Tony Hoffman;
Talk About Man Proof - Lancelot Runge / John Kropa; An Admission as a Warning Against the Value of Our Conclusions -Alexis Quinlan

DOC U MENT
/däky ə m ə nt/
First meant "instruction" or "evidence," whether written or not.

> *noun* - a piece of written, printed, or electronic matter that provides information or evidence or that serves as an official record
> *verb* - record (something) in written, photographic, or other form
> *synonyms* - paper - deed - record - writing - act - instrument
>
> [*Middle English, precept, from Old French, from Latin documentum, example, proof, from docre, to teach; see dek- in Indo-European roots.*]

Who is responsible for the manufacture of value?

Based on what supercilious ontology have we landed in a space where we vie against other creative people in vain pursuit of the fleeting credibilities of the scarcity economy, rather than freely collaborating and sharing openly with each other in ecstatic celebration of MAKING?

While we understand and acknowledge the economic pressures and fear-mongering that threatens to dominate and crush the creative impulse, we also believe that ***now more than ever we have the tools to relinquish agency via cooperative means,*** fueled by the fires of the Open Source Movement.

Looking out across the invisible vistas of that rhizomatic parallel country we can begin to see our community beyond constraints, in the place where intention meets resilient, proactive, collaborative organization.

Here is a document born of that belief, sown purely of imagination and will.
When we document we assert.
We print to make real, to reify our being there.
When we do so with mindful intention to address our process,
to open our work to others, to create beauty in words in space, to respect and acknowledge the strength of the page we now hold physical,
a thing in our hand… we remind ourselves that, like Dorothy:
we had the power all along, my dears.

THE PRINT! DOCUMENT SERIES
is a project of the trouble with bartleby
in collaboration with
the operating system

www.ingramcontent.com/pod-product-compliance
Lightning Source LLC
Chambersburg PA
CBHW021453080526
44588CB00009B/822